MODERN BUSINESS LETTERS
70 Ready-to-Use Models
Second Edition

Joan Harris

Asher-Gallant Press
Westbury, New York • New York

Asher-Gallant Press is a division of Caddylak Systems, Inc. Address all inquiries to Asher-Gallant Press, 201 Montrose Road, Westbury, New York 11590, or call (516) 333-8221.

Library of Congress Cataloging in Publication Data

Harris, Joan.
    Modern business letters.

    1. Commercial correspondence—Handbooks, manuals, etc.
2. Form letters—Handbooks, manuals, etc.   3. Customer
relations—Handbooks, manuals, etc.   I. Title.
HF5726.H336   1985   651.7'52   85-3825
ISBN 0-87280-998-6

Printed in the United States of America

Table of Contents

Introduction

Any business executive knows that good business letters are important. The business letter is an indispensable tool in almost any company. A good business letter not only will do the obvious task for which it is written—acknowledging an order, soothing an angry customer, transmitting information—it also will sell the company as a comfortable one with which to do business. Every business letter should promote your image.

Good business letters can encourage additional sales by cementing relationships between you and the customer or supplier to whom you are writing. Don't believe it? Compare these two letters answering a customer complaint:

Dear Sir:

Regarding your letter or complaint dated June 5, be assured that we are investigating the circumstances of your unfortunate experience. We would like to apologize, and we are enclosing a $5 gift certificate good for any future orders.

Very truly yours,

Dear Mr. Johnson:

I was very sorry to hear of your unfortunate experience with our mail order department.

Let me assure you that we value our customers and that such rudeness as you experienced is inexcusable. I have asked Harry Smith, the department manager, to investigate the circumstances of your complaint. He is to report to me within the week on what action he has taken to make sure the problem does not recur.

I appreciate your taking the time to write and let me know about your problem so that we can correct it. I am enclosing a

$5 gift certificate as partial compensation for your unhappy experience.

Once again, I would like to apologize for this very unusual slip-up and emphasize how much we value your continued patronage.

Very truly yours,

There's only one reason for responding to any customer complaint of this type. That's to keep the writer as your customer. Which letter do you think will be more likely to encourage Mr. Johnson to try again with this company?

If you picked the second letter, you are in agreement with most modern experts on business and business writing. Why will the letter be more effective? It's because it sounds more sincere, more personal.

The first letter sounds like a form letter, churned out mechanically without any concern for the problem. It doesn't even restate the problem; it's so vague that it could be used to respond to any number of customer complaints. And don't think the customer doesn't realize it! The first letter sounds like the company really couldn't care less.

The second letter, on the other hand, sounds like someone read, understood, and took action on the customer's complaint. It clearly restates the complaint, and endorses it as valid. It outlines what action the company took. It apologizes for the problem, thanks the customer for his time and interest, and encourages future orders. It does all that without sounding sappy—a too-apologetic letter can sound insincere and make your company look silly. The message of the second letter is clear: We are interested in you. We value your patronage. Such a letter is far more likely to buy continued goodwill than a $5 gift certificate accompanied by an assembly-line apology.

Certainly impersonal, form-type letters are easier and quicker to write. However, common sense will tell you that a letter that saves time but loses the customer is no savings at all. Why not take an extra couple of minutes to make your letter a sales tool? Include a personal note or suggestion that tells the reader that your company sees him or her as more than just someone who helps you make money.

When acknowledging an order, suggest another line of products in which your customer may be interested. If you have to tell a customer that you're out of stock on an item, recommend another item to replace it. If a prospective customer asks for a catalog, propose an appointment with one of your sales representatives. If you have to write a dunning letter for an overdue bill—surely one of the most unpleasant tasks in business—ask the customer whether you can help by arranging an extended-payments schedule. When writing to a long-time customer or supplier, include some personal good wishes.

Thoughtful, personal communications with colleagues and members of the community are equally important. If you can accept or decline a speaking engagement gracefully, or write a meaningful condolence or congratulatory letter to a colleague, you will increase the respect that others have for you.

Taking the time to communicate personally with the people to whom you write is a form of advertising. It tells them you're sincerely interested in continuing the relationship. It tells them you value them.

Good business letters are not easy to write. That's where this book can help you. It includes 70 sample letters covering a wide variety of business subjects that you can use as models for your own communications. Each letter includes detailed marginal notes to guide you in revising the letter for your own particular needs. Use these models to help you write letters that sell your company's image—and your own.

Letter-Writing Tips

• The most effective letters are those written in simple, clear language. Strive for a conversational style rather than stilted business boilerplate like "as per your letter of the 12th, we are not prepared to interface at this time, pending determination of . . ." Keep your sentence structure simple and your paragraphs short. Don't overwrite; get to the point of your letter quickly and stay on it.

• "You" is a popular word with most readers; use it as often as possible. Use "I" when referring to yourself, either as an individual or as a spokesman for your company. Use "we" when referring to your entire company. ("On behalf of Welbilt Corp., I would like to welcome you as a new customer. We will do our best to keep you happy.")

• When addressing correspondents, the goal is to be friendly but not overly familiar. Don't use first names too freely.

• Remember that readers are interested in their problems, not yours. If there is a particular reason for a service problem (for instance, if your company has recently moved), mention it as an explanation, not an excuse. A dissatisfied customer will still expect an apology and an effort to make things right. It costs nothing to say "I'm sorry."

• If you have good news to impart, trumpet it at the start of your letter. On the other hand, if you have bad news, don't make the reader wade through four paragraphs before he or she gets to your point. Instead of trying to hide it, state your bad news sensitively, offsetting it with a positive statement. Examples: "We are forced to raise prices eight percent to maintain the high quality of our products"; "We are out of stock on the line you ordered, but I would like to suggest some alternative products."

• Your letters should be self-contained, meaning that the reader should not have to refer to an earlier letter or invoice to determine what you're talking about. Restating the problem or the order also gives the reader confirmation that you understand his or her needs.

• When writing letters acknowledging personal milestones, such as a marriage, a promotion, or a birth in the family, be especially careful to say something personal and sincere. If you have any difficulties in this area, send a card rather than a letter.

• Answer your mail promptly. A quick response is additional proof that you care about your correspondent.

• To increase efficiency, your company should have a standard format for writing letters. It should specify such things as whether all parts of the letter (the date, recipient's address, salutation, body, complimentary close, and signature) are flush left or indented, what salutations are preferred, and how the signature line should look.

MODEL LETTERS

First Reminder Letter

**State amount due and
number of days late.**

Dear _____ :

According to our records, the balance of
$_____ on your account is now _____
past due.

**Assume the customer
intends to pay.**

Since this is an unusual occurrence, we assume
it is an oversight. If, however, there is a
particular reason why you haven't paid your bill
on time, please call us so we can discuss it.

**Reduce annoyance factor
in case the customer has
paid.**

In case you've already sent us a check, please
disregard our reminder.

Thank you.

Sincerely,

Second Reminder Letter

Dear ——————— :

State amount due and number of days late.

Your balance of $———— is now —— days past due. This is our second reminder.

Assume that the customer intends to pay.

If your overdue account is merely an oversight, we hope you will take care of this matter right away.

Ask the customer to contact you to work out any problems.

If there are special circumstances, or if you are dissatisfied with our service for some reason, please write or call us so that we can work things out.

Indicate when you expect the check.

We will expect to receive either a check or some other reply from you by ————.

Reassure the customer of your continued respect.

You are a valued customer and we would like our relationship with you to continue. Be assured that we will do our best to work out any problems you may have.

Sincerely,

Third Reminder Letter

State amount due and number of days late.

Dear _____ :

We again find it necessary to remind you of the past-due balance of $_____ on your account. This amount has been due us since _____, and this is our third past-due request.

Point out that you have tried to be considerate and the customer has not responded.

In our last letter about this matter, we asked you to let us know by _____ whether there was some problem that was preventing you from paying. We have not yet received a response.

Explain your next step.

Unless we receive payment immediately, we will have to refer your account to our collection department. As you know, this will have a serious adverse effect on your credit rating.

Indicate that you hope to work things out and make the new deadline clear.

We have considered you a valued customer, and would prefer not to have to take this step. We expect to receive your check by _____.

Thank you.

Sincerely,

Final Reminder Letter

Dear _____ :

Start with a statement about the lawsuit to get your customer's attention. Restate the details.

Our collection department has informed me that it intends to file suit to recover the $_____ that you have owed us since _____ . This action is being taken because you have not responded to our three previous payment requests.

Give the customer one last chance before filing suit. Make it clear that this is the last time you will ask.

Before we begin legal action, I would like to make one final personal appeal for you to call me. We have appreciated the business you have given us, and I am sure that we can find some way to settle this out of court.

Be specific as to when you will take action.

Please telephone me by _____ so that we can avoid the unpleasantness of a lawsuit.

Sincerely,

11

Letter Correcting a Company Error

Describe the error and thank the customer for bringing it to your attention.

Dear ———————— :

Thank you for your letter of April 30 telling us that we sent you 100 copies of Easy-to-Make Graphs and Charts instead of the 100 copies of Easy-to-Make Data and Columnar Sheets you ordered.

Explain how you have corrected the error.

You already should have received the correct shipment, which we sent to you by Federal Express the day we received your letter. In this letter, we are enclosing a check for $————————, which should cover the cost of shipping the incorrect order back to us.

Apologize for the mistake.

Let me offer our apologies for our mistake. I hope the delay did not inconvenience you.

End on a positive note about future business.

We make shipping mistakes rarely, but when we do make an error we do everything we can to solve the problem immediately. We hope the steps we took are satisfactory to you, and we look forward to continuing our relationship.

Sincerely,

Credit Approval Letter

Dear _____ :

Welcome the reader as a new credit customer.

Our credit department has just approved your application. It's a pleasure to welcome you as a Hanover credit customer!

Detail the first order and give shipping information.

We will ship your first order of _____ on Wednesday, May 4. You should receive it by May 9.

Explain your credit policy.

We will send you a statement on the first of each month, reflecting the previous month's orders. Your payment, in full, is due by the tenth of each month. Along with your statement, we will send you new-product announcements as well as order forms and envelopes.

Tell the customer how to contact you (the salesperson). If appropriate, suggest a face-to-face meeting.

If you have any questions regarding products, shipments, pricing, scheduling, etc., please call me collect any weekday between 9 a.m. and noon. In addition, I'd like to meet with you to discuss our products and make suggestions as to how we can best serve you. Why not call me to set up an appointment?

Reassure the customer of your intention to please.

We are sure our products will bring you added sales and profits, and we look forward to a long and mutually prosperous business relationship.

Sincerely,

Credit Refusal Letter

Dear _____ :

Thank the customer for the credit application.

Thank you for your interest in our company, as expressed by your recent credit application.

State your refusal and explain your reasoning.

Unfortunately, we find we cannot extend credit to you at this time. Our routine investigation of your financial situation shows us that your current obligations are substantial. We believe that if you add to these obligations you may endanger your credit standing.

Remind the customer that you can still do business.

Naturally, we'd be happy to ship you any of our products on a C.O.D. basis. We certainly would like to have you as a customer.

Keep the credit option open.

If in the future there is a change in your credit responsibilities, please let us know so that we can reconsider your credit application.

Thank you.

Sincerely,

Letter Approving an Adjustment

Dear _____:

Thank the customer for the letter and state your decision.

Thank you for your letter of May 14. We are sorry you are dissatisfied, and we will be glad to take back the shipment of Model 228 pencil sharpeners and credit your account.

Explain the reason for the problem, if you can.

We described the design changes we made in the Model 228 in our latest catalog, but we understand that you might not have thought to read about a product you have ordered routinely for several years.

Tell the customer how to return the shipment.

If you are certain you want to return the shipment, please send it back to us as quickly as possible. We'll be happy to send you a check to cover the freight charges.

If appropriate, make a sales pitch.

We would recommend, however, that you reconsider and give the new model a try on your shelves. We changed the design to make the pencil sharpener operate more efficiently, take up less space, and blend in better with today's modern office designs. Many of our vendors have found that sales have increased since the design change, and we believe that you would, too.

Sincerely,

Letter Refusing an Adjustment

Dear _____ :

Acknowledge the customer's request and state your decision.

We received your letter today asking us to take back the paper order we sent you on May 4. We have always tried to honor your requests, but we regret that we are unable to do so now.

Explain how your company has tried to meet the customer's needs. Avoid being combative or condescending.

When we found that we could no longer offer our customers the 2211 grade paper, we sent out letters explaining this. We also sent out a thorough description of the new 2311 paper we are offering instead. When we sent the brochure about the 2311 paper a month ago, we encouraged you to make an appointment with one of our sales representatives to see a sample of the new paper and discuss its qualities. We did our best to make all our customers familiar with the paper's features before they ordered it.

State why you must refuse.

Because of the size of your order and the cost of the shipment, we simply cannot afford to take it back.

Make one more sales pitch. Indicate that you are still willing to help.

We hope you understand our position. We would recommend strongly that you give this new paper a try. Most of our customers have said they are pleased with it, telling us that the paper appeared stronger, the type clearer, and the overall quality slightly better than the 2211.

Close on a positive note.

We are confident that, if you give it a chance, you will feel the same way. If you have any questions about the use of the paper, please call us.

Sincerely,

Letter Offering a Compromise

Dear _____:

Acknowledge the letter and sympathize with the customer's position.

We have received your letter of June 23, and we are sorry that you are dissatisfied with the 2311 paper that we sent you.

Explain the reason for your refusal. Restate your position if necessary.

As we explained in our May 1 notice, we can no longer supply our customers with the 2211 grade of paper you have used for the past five years, but we sincerely believe that the 2311 paper offers superior results for printing catalogs and brochures.

Because you've already used your order to print your summer catalog, we don't feel we should credit your account for the full amount of $_____, as you requested.

Offer the compromise in positive terms.

We would, however, like to offer you a compromise. As soon as we receive payment for the 2311 paper already used, we will offer you a 25% discount on your next order over $_____.

Show the customer that his or her satisfaction is important. Tell what you will do to ensure satisfaction.

A sales representative will set up an appointment with you to make sure you will be pleased with the next paper you choose. We hope you find this compromise fair, and we look forward to hearing from you.

Sincerely,

Letter Refusing a Request

Dear _____:

Thank the customer for the letter and the order.

Thank you for your letter of May 15 requesting immediate delivery of 300 cases of our new, unbreakable glassware.

Explain why you cannot grant the request.

Our spring catalog announced this product as being available by July 1. This means that we could not ship your order before then.

Tell what you are doing to meet the customer's needs.

We have processed your order and put you on a preferred-delivery list. This means your glassware will be shipped to you the day it's put into inventory. We are certain that you will receive your order by July 7.

Make a sales pitch or offer an alternative, if appropriate.

In the meantime, you might consider taking advantage of a new 33% price reduction on our line of unbreakable mugs. These are available for ten-day delivery.

Indicate that you care about the customer's satisfaction.

We will make every effort to get your unbreakable glassware to you as soon as possible.

Sincerely,

Inquiry Letter

Dear _____ :

Give the reason for your inquiry. Explain how you know about the company or service.

We would like to investigate the possibility of holding a sales convention at your hotel. The hotel was recommended to us by Ray Harris of Hufco Corporation, which held its Christmas party there last year. He was impressed with the quality of your service.

Detail your needs.

Our sales convention this year will fall on the weekend of June 5. Forty sales representatives and their spouses will meet to see our new products and celebrate the year's successes.

Be very specific.

We plan to start our weekend about 11 a.m. Friday and to leave about 4 p.m. Sunday.

We will need 40 double rooms, equal in size and quality, and we would like to reserve tables in your dining room for all meals from Friday luncheon to Sunday luncheon. Further, we will need a private room for a cocktail party on Saturday evening from 5 p.m. to 7 p.m. We also will need a conference room all day Saturday and through 2 p.m. on Sunday.

For recreation, we'd like unlimited use of your tennis courts and pool. We also would ask you to schedule eight foursomes on your golf course at 8 a.m. Sunday.

State how and when you should be contacted.

Please call me as soon as possible to let me know whether you can meet these requirements. We will need to know your rates for rooms, meals, and meeting facilities.

Be positive about the outcome.

I look forward to working with you.

Sincerely,

Letter Placing an Order

Dear _____ :

Explain the reason for your letter.

Thank you for sending us your spring catalog. We would like to order two of your products.

Give all the details, including desired delivery date.

Please ship us, mailed C.O.D., 50 copies of book #306 at $9.95 each, and 75 copies of book #307, at $10.95 each. We would like to receive these books by June 1. Please let us know immediately if you are unable to deliver by that date.

Make any further requests. Express positive feelings about future business.

Also, please send us a credit application so that we can arrange to charge subsequent orders. We expect to do more business in the future.

Thank you.

Sincerely,

Letter Requesting Reservations

Give names, dates, and times. Be specific about what you want.

Detail any special requests.

State when you expect confirmation.

Dear ——————— :

We would like to reserve a deluxe one-bedroom suite for our senior vice president, Mr. Donald Diamond, on Friday and Saturday, June 1 and 2. He expects to check in by 8 p.m. Friday and to check out by 3 p.m. Sunday.

In addition, he would like to reserve your small conference room on Saturday from 10 a.m. to 1 p.m. We would like you to provide coffee and danish for 20 people during this meeting.

Please confirm these reservations, specifying prices for all services, by May 10.

Thank you.

Sincerely,

Acknowledgment Letter

Thank the person for the information.

Dear _____ :

Thank you for sending me Sally Germain's resume. You were right when you said her editorial experience and merchandising background seemed like a good fit for the special assistant's job we're trying to fill.

Detail the next step.

I'll call you sometime next week to set up a time for Sally to come in and meet with our four department heads.

Sincerely yours,

Follow-up Letter

Dear ———————:

State reason for correspondence.

I'm thrilled that you've agreed to speak at our annual Sports Day on June 18. I know your scheduled appearance will help us sell even more tickets than last year!

Give details on project or issue.

As I told you on the phone, your talk will be scheduled first, at 2 p.m. This will enable you to make that 5 p.m. flight to Washington. I've arranged to have someone from the office drive you to the airport.

Explain what you expect from the reader.

Please prepare a 45-minute presentation. We'll allow another half hour for questions and answers. Lunch will start promptly at noon, and you'll begin right afterward.

State when you will communicate with him or her next.

I look forward to seeing you then and will call you by June 10 to discuss the details of the day.

Sincerely yours,

Appointment Confirmation Letter

Dear _____ :

Explain what you are confirming.

I'm writing to confirm our May 16 appointment to discuss your services. We will meet you in the small conference room on the second floor at 2 p.m.

Make any additional points.

I've arranged to have my purchasing agents and the entire sales force attend your presentation, so please be prompt.

Spell out the reader's responsibilities and yours.

We'll supply the 16mm projector. You will supply us with your ten-minute film and another twenty minutes of information to help us make this decision.

Ask for additional input. Reaffirm positive feelings.

We look forward to seeing you then. Please let me know if there's anything special you'd like me to do to ensure a smooth and productive meeting.

Sincerely yours,

Remittance Letter

Dear _____ :

State amount of payment and invoice number.

The enclosed check for _____ is in payment of invoice # _____ . Please credit our account for this amount.

Give statement of account status.

Our records indicate that this payment will bring us completely up to date as of your last statement of _____ .

Sincerely yours,

Stopgap Letter

Dear _____ :

Acknowledge letter.

Your invitation to Dan Smythe to attend your annual Spring Physical Fitness weekend arrived this morning.

Explain why person is unable to respond.

Dan is out of town and is expected back sometime during the week of May ____.

Reassure the reader that the person will respond as soon as possible.

I'll make sure that Dan sees your letter as soon as he returns. I know you will hear from him sometime that week.

Sincerely yours,

Inquiry Letter

Dear _____:

Thank the reader for his or her inquiry and interest.

Thank you for your interest in Fitness First. We've enclosed a brochure which describes our philosophy, classes, and facilities and shows you a complete weekly schedule.

Answer the reader's requests in detail.

Since we offer ten classes a day, we're confident you can make exercise a routine part of your daily schedule.

We charge $3.75 for your first class and $7.50 per class after that. However, most of our members attend at least three classes a week and save more than 50% by buying our monthly unlimited membership card.

Sell your service or product. Invite the reader's business.

We invite you to join us for a class soon. We're sure you'll find Fitness First a satisfying, comfortable, and enjoyable place to get into shape.

Sincerely yours,

Order Acknowledgment Letter

Thank the customer for the order. Add a positive comment specific to the order.

Restate details of the order, and give the invoice amount, the expected delivery date, and the payment terms.

Start selling the customer on another order.

Include sales aids or other ideas.

Dear _____:

Thank you for your order of May 12 (invoice #_____). We know you'll be happy to hear that the unitards you've requested have become a best-seller across the country in just the first month they have been available.

You will receive six dozen hot pink (#202), three dozen turquoise-and-white-striped (#204), and three dozen multicolored (#205) pair on or before June 15. Our invoice, which will include shipping costs, will be attached to this order. The full amount of $_____ is due ten days after you've received the merchandise.

Our winter line of leg warmers and dance pants is quite spectacular this year. Annette Johnson will stop by within the next two weeks to show you samples and help you with your next order.

We are enclosing some photographs to give you ideas for displaying your unitards on the sales floor and in your windows.

Sincerely yours,

Order Referral Letter

Dear _____ :

Thank the customer for the order and explain why you must make a referral.

Thank you for your order for one pair of royal blue running shorts and matching shirt. However, as a manufacturer of running clothes, we are not set up to sell directly to the customer.

State what you've done to take care of the request.

We've passed your letter to the U.S. Running Shop in your town, which carries our full line of sports clothes. A representative of that store will contact you to find out if you want the order sent to you. You might prefer to pick it up yourself.

Thank the customer again for his or her interest.

Thank you for your interest in our products.

Sincerely yours,

Order Refusal Letter

Dear _____ :

Thank the customer for his or her interest.

Thank you for your October 1 order of eight dozen pair of running shorts.

Explain that you cannot fulfill the order, and tell why.

Since 1962, when we began manufacturing a full line of running and exercise clothes, we've sold only to those retailers that carry our entire line. Therefore, we are unable to fill an order only for running shorts.

We spend a lot of money on national advertising and find that stores benefit tremendously by offering our entire line. Our advertising encourages consumers to outfit themselves completely with our products. If you were to offer only our shorts, your customer would have to look elsewhere for our jackets, warm-up suits, T-shirts, socks, headbands, visors, and other products.

Suggest an alternative. Do a selling job.

Why don't you consider carrying our full line? One of our sales representatives, Bob Stone, will call you to discuss this idea. He will give you our special introductory offer of a 10% discount on your first order over $500, and will detail our co-op advertising plan.

Express hope for future business.

We hope we'll be able to add you to our list of satisfied and successful dealers.

Sincerely,

Notice of Price Increase

Dear _____ :

Make a positive statement about your product.

You know that the rubber we use to make our tires is outstanding. That's why you order from us, and that's why your customers ask for our tires by name.

Give the amount, effective date, and reason for the increase.

Unfortunately, because of recent increases in the cost of U.S.-made rubber, we will have to raise our prices about 8%, effective September 1. Because quality remains our first concern, we want to continue to use U.S.-made rubber, rather than less expensive imported rubber.

Apologize for the necessity of the increase. Assure the customer of your product's value.

We're sorry that this price increase is necessary. But we're sure you understand that we have to do it in order to continue to offer you the top-quality tires you've come to expect from us.

Sincerely yours,

Notice of Price Reduction

Give the good news.

Dear _____ :

I am delighted to say that we are cutting the price of our USB Video Tape Recorder (Model 83R).

Explain the details of and reason for the reduction.

Because of the phenomenal sales of this model in 1984, we can save you 10% on all future orders for 1985.

Tell customers that they share responsibility for the good news.

Stores like yours have helped make this reduction possible. You've promoted and sold our product effectively and successfully.

Thank you for your help!

Sincerely,

New Office Announcement

Dear _____ :

Give the date of move, address, and phone number.

We're delighted to announce the opening of our new office at _____. We're moving to this address on June 17 and will be ready for business as of June 22. For your convenience, our telephone number will remain the same.

Thank customers for their part in the move. Show how they will benefit.

Thank you for contributing to our success. Our new prosperity has allowed us to take over twice as much space and to hire seven additional order processors. This new setup will benefit you with increased efficiency and faster service.

Give invitation details if applicable.

Please join us to celebrate this move on June 28 at 7 p.m. for cocktails and hors d'oeuvres. We're proud of our beautiful new quarters and want to share them with our very best customers.

Sincerely yours,

Vacation Shutdown Announcement

Dear _____ :

Give dates of shutdown.

It is again time for our plant's annual vacation week. We will be closed from June 15 through June 22.

Reassure customers that it won't affect their business.

Naturally, we don't want to let this affect your company's operation. We'll make sure that all your July orders are filled and delivered by our first vacation day.

Explain what you need from them.

To make this possible, we ask you to send us your July order by June 1.

Add any other relevant information.

As always, our business office will remain open every day from 9 a.m. to 5 p.m.

Thank you for your cooperation.

Sincerely yours,

Letter Following Up a Prospect Lead

Dear ＿＿＿＿＿＿＿ :

Name the person who made the referral. Create interest.

Ann Jacobs suggested that I contact you to explain my special service. When I asked her to name the hardest-working executives she knows, your name was high on her list.

Explain your service or product.

I am an executive shopper. I buy gifts for businesspeople to send to clients, friends, and relatives. My customers are busy executives who can't spare the time to deal with crowded stores, long gift-wrap lines, and difficult gift decisions.

Sell the idea. Show how the prospect will benefit from it.

I specialize in unusual ideas. People remember the gifts I choose as being just what they wanted. I assure you that I will always buy gifts of which you would approve.

With Christmas just three months away, I'd like to meet with you to discuss how I can make this season more enjoyable for you and all the people on your list.

Mention price.

You will be amazed at how little it will cost to have me do a job that robs you of precious time, that you dread doing year after year.

(continued on following page)

Tell the prospect you will contact him or her.

I'll call you next week to set up an appointment. I hope you will let me help you out this Christmas season.

Sincerely yours,

Letter Seeking to Reactivate an Account

	Dear ＿＿＿＿＿＿＿ :
Attract attention.	You are important to us!
Tell the customer how he or she is important to you.	In this computer age, many companies see their customers as simply another line on a printout sheet. But at ＿＿＿＿＿＿＿, we don't feel that way. You've been a good customer, and we want you to continue to do business with us.
Tell the customer how long the account has been inactive. Ask why you haven't heard from him or her.	We've noticed that your account has been inactive since ＿＿＿＿＿. We'd like to know, quite simply, what happened to put our relationship on hold. Have there been problems with your previous orders that we've been unaware of? Has your business situation changed in a significant way? Have you been dissatisfied in any way with our service or our product?
Tell the customer how to respond to your inquiry.	Please take a moment or two to fill out the enclosed card and return it to us so we can find out why we haven't heard from you.
Remind the customer of his or her importance.	We want to keep you as a customer. Please tell us how we can satisfy you, how we can improve our relationship. We look forward to hearing from you soon. Remember, you are important to us!
	Sincerely,

Letter Making a Business Referral

Dear _____ :

Tell the reader who or what you are referring.

I'd like to recommend Leslie Stark for the PR work on that new product you told me about.

Explain why this person, service, or product is worthwhile.

Last year, when we launched the "Mary, The Female Astronaut" doll, we hired Leslie for the first time. Not only does she have more energy and creativity than anyone else we've worked with in the toy industry, but her connections with the media are solid.

She got us two national features and a network plug in the first week alone. I give her much of the credit for "Mary's" initial success. We've never had a major department-store run on any doll like we did that first month.

Create more interest.

I'm only giving you Leslie's name because I owe you a favor! Please don't pass it on to other companies—I plan to keep her busy this September and I want her to be available.

Sincerely,

Letter Soliciting Inquiries

Arouse the reader's interest in the product or service.

Dear _____ :

You've heard about Natural Sweet on television. You've read about Natural Sweet in every major newspaper and magazine. You've been told it's not available to the consumer. You've learned it contains absolutely no artificial ingredients. You've noted it has only one calorie per teaspoonful.

You've wanted to buy it but you couldn't.

Invite the reader to find out more.

Do you want to know more about this wonder product? Do you want to find out when it will be in stores for you to buy and bring home? Do you want to try a sample and see for yourself that it tastes exactly like sugar?

Tell the reader how to contact you and what he or she can expect.

Then fill out the enclosed coupon. We'll send you our brochure and a free sample right away.

Natural Sweet is finally on its way to your kitchen. You won't be disappointed!

Sincerely yours,

Sales Appointment Letter

Dear _____ :

An intriguing question is often an effective opener.

Who are your best employees—the ones who get to work on time, seem calm even when facing a crisis, and get along best with their co-workers and clients? What do they have in common?

Introduce your service or product. If appropriate, tell a little bit about your company.

Most likely, your best employees are your physically fit employees. How do we know this? Because we're Fitness First, a group of fitness experts who specialize in setting up employee physical fitness programs for businesses such as yours.

Mention some of the benefits of your service/ product. Tell how your service/product will benefit the reader.

Regular exercise has been proven to increase productivity in working people. In fact, medical experts are so sure that physically fit people make the best employees that they have begun to convince insurance companies of it. And now, your insurance company is willing to lower your premium rates if you can prove that your employees exercise regularly.

Consolidated Life Insurance has agreed to drop your insurance rates 17% if you can guarantee that 72% of your employees engage in regular physical exercise—just four times a week, an hour at a time. With an exercise program designed specifically for your company by our staff of health and fitness experts, that 17% savings is virtually assured.

Restate the benefits.

Wouldn't it be great to see increased productivity and enthusiasm at your company? And wouldn't you like to use that 17% savings toward something that would increase profits—new product development, for instance?

Spell out the purpose of your letter (to set up a meeting). Mention other firms that have already benefited from your service/product.

We would like to come in to discuss how Fitness First can tailor a physical fitness program for your company—as it has for over 35 Long Island-based clients of Consolidated in the past year alone. We'd like just an hour of your time—an hour we know will be meaningful to you in the future.

Tell the reader you will contact him or her, and when.

We'll be calling you next week for an appointment.

Sincerely,

Creative Sales Letter

Use the salutation to target your audience.

Dear Manager:

Begin with a statement or question that will spark interest.

Suppose you could increase your secretary's productivity by 33 percent.

Show why the reader needs your product. (Gimmicks such as underlining, highlighting with different colors, and indenting important paragraphs can be effective if used sparingly.)

Studies show that much of your secretary's time is nonproductive. Experts have determined that he or she spends up to one-third of the workday doing dull, repetitive tasks—typing letters over and over for minor changes, typing the same addresses and standard paragraphs again and again. Think how much more your secretary could accomplish for you if he or she could be freed from this wasteful routine!

Continue to sell your product. Point out its special features. Explain in the simplest possible terms how it works.

Well, that freedom is here, thanks to the Autowriter line of electronic typewriters from Franklin Business Machines. With these impressive new machines, you can have a word processor for the price of a typewriter. The Autowriter can store up to 300 pages of text in its memory. Your secretary can type a letter, you can change it or correct it, and he or she can print a completely revised copy for you almost instantly—at a rate of 170 words per minute.

By simply pressing four buttons, your secretary can print out up to 199 different addresses or stock paragraphs, perfect every time. And as your business grows, your Autowriter can grow with it. Additional memory capacity is available that can hold up to <u>600</u> pages of text.

After you've explained why the product is necessary, persuade the reader to buy it at <u>your</u> store.

An Autowriter typewriter will give you years of reliable service, backed by Franklin's good name and better guarantee. And, since we are the regional service center for these fine machines, you can be assured that your office will keep running smoothly.

Add a sense of urgency to the letter. Tell the reader what you want him or her to do about your offer.

For a limited time only, we are able to offer the Franklin Autowriter line of electronic type-writers at a special low price. <u>We guarantee that our prices are the lowest in the area for these or any comparable electronic typewriters.</u> Why not come in and see our line today?

Sincerely yours,

The "P.S." is one of the best-read parts of a sales letter. Give your readers something meaningful.

P.S. Why not drop in soon and see the electronic typewriters <u>Workplace Automation</u> magazine called "the best value in word processing today"?

Letter Responding to Customer Criticism

Dear _____ :

Acknowledge the letter and show concern for the customer's feelings.

We're sorry to hear that a good customer like you is unhappy with our policy of shortened summer hours.

Explain the reason for the policy that was criticized.

Your letter of complaint arrived this morning and I wanted to send you an explanation right away. First, about half our regular customers go away weekends between Memorial Day and Labor Day. This makes it less profitable for us to stay open on Saturdays and Sundays. Further, since our employees regularly work weekends during the fall, winter, and spring months, we welcome the opportunity to let them enjoy their summer weekends.

If feasible, offer the customer an alternative to resolve the problem.

Is there something special we could do to make the adjustment easier? We would be happy to accept mail or phone orders from you and ship the merchandise C.O.D. If you would find such an arrangement convenient, please give me a call.

Show your desire to please the customer.

We value your patronage, and we would like to accommodate you any way we can.

Sincerely yours,

Letter Apologizing for a Company Error

Dear _____ :

Apologize for the error.

We regret to say that there is a major typographic error in our spring catalog.

Explain the error.

The purple and white tiger tulip bulbs (#3078), imported from Holland, cost $1.50 each, not $0.15, as printed.

Explain how you plan to correct it.

If we receive an order from you that includes these bulbs, we'll return it so you can reorder at the correct price. Naturally, we'll make sure there's no delay in getting the amended order to you in plenty of time for planting.

Make a positive sales pitch.

Even at a price of $1.50 each, we're offering these prize-winning tulips at more than 20% less than any other import house in the United States.

Sincerely yours,

Letter Apologizing for Company Discourtesy

Dear _____ :

Thank the customer for his or her letter.

Thank you for your recent letter expressing dissatisfaction with the phone manners of our order department personnel.

Apologize for the problem and thank the customer for telling you about it.

I am very sorry that you were displeased, and I want to thank you for bringing the situation to my attention so I could take action to correct it.

Explain what you did about the complaint. If you detail extenuating circumstances, make clear that you don't accept them as excuses.

The day after I received your letter, I met with my order department supervisors. They told me that last month was not only the busiest time ever for phone orders, but was also an inopportune time for the air conditioning to break down.

Restate your commitment to courtesy. Reassure the customer that the problem won't happen again.

Although we could all understand why the attitude of some employees was not up to par, we agreed that there is no excuse for discourtesy to customers. I plan to meet with all of our order personnel to personally restate our commitment to courtesy and helpfulness. All of us want to apologize for your unpleasant experience and assure you that it will not recur.

Show that you were pleased to receive the complaint.

Thank you again for letting me know that a problem existed. I hope you will communicate again if you are ever less than completely satisfied with us.

Sincerely yours,

Letter Answering an Unsolicited Suggestion

Dear _____ :

Thank the writer for his or her letter and suggestion.

Thank you very much for your suggestion about packaging our dessert glasses with our wine and cordial assortment.

Explain what you plan to do about the idea (or why you cannot try it).

We are extremely interested in your idea. I've passed your letter on to the research and design team to look into the feasibility of such a combination. If we decide to test this package, would you be willing to serve as our New York "guinea pig" and carry about 50 sets in the fall?

Show the writer how pleased you are with his or her input.

I'll keep in touch with you and let you know what we decide. Thanks again for your interest and enthusiasm, and for an especially creative idea.

Sincerely yours,

Letter Announcing a Bonus/ Promotion for Customers

Dear _____ :

Tell the customer you have some good news.	We have some good news for our very best customers!
Thank the customer for being a good customer, and define that category.	You, of course, fit into that category. You place your orders on time, consistently order more than $3,000 of merchandise each month, and pay your bills within the discount period.
Explain the bonus or promotion.	We've decided, as a bonus, to offer you free delivery. If you check your delivery charges on previous bills, you'll find this will save you about $500 a year.
Explain how it will work.	This new service won't affect your delivery date at all. The only difference is that as long as you continue to be a good customer, we, not you, pay the delivery charge.
Thank the customer again.	Thanks again for being such a special customer year after year.

Sincerely yours,

Holiday Note to Customers and Associates

Dear _____ :

Let the reader know he or she is more to you than just a business associate.

The holidays give me an opportunity to write to you about feelings rather than business-related matters. This is especially meaningful to me because I know our relationship is based on something more than just a common interest in my products and your business.

Make your letter a personal one. (If this is impractical, send cards instead.)

Of course I truly appreciate the business you've given us over the past 12 years. But even more, I've enjoyed the conversation during our lunches together and the joint service we've had this year on the Community Fund Drive.

Wish the reader a happy holiday.

I hope your Christmas and New Year holidays are filled with good spirits and joy, and I wish you, Tina, and the children all the best for a happy and prosperous 1985.

Reinforce the personal relationship with the reader.

I look forward to a continued relationship with you and to the good feelings we share each day of the year.

Sincerely yours,

Letter Offering Congratulations

Dear _____ :

Give the reason for the congratulatory letter.

Congratulations! I just heard that you've added the Americo Toy Company to your long list of clients.

Comment on why the person deserves congratulations.

I can't say I'm surprised. I've always known you were the best advertising agency around. Why else would I continue to give you all my business—and my trust—year after year?

If the relationship calls for it, suggest a way to celebrate.

Let's get together for a celebration lunch sometime next week. I'd like an opportunity to toast you in person.

Best wishes,

Letter Expressing Appreciation

Dear _____ :

Explain the reason for the note and say thanks.

Thank you very much for recommending me to Sean Harris to write his autobiography. We're meeting next Thursday to discuss the details.

Show your appreciation.

I can't imagine a stronger vote of confidence from you than a recommendation to someone of Mr. Harris's stature.

If appropriate, suggest a further way to show your appreciation.

May I take you to lunch next week to show my appreciation? I'll give you a call in a couple of days to make plans.

Best wishes,

Congratulatory Letter—Anniversary

The feelings you convey are more important than what you say.

Use a warm, enthusiastic, and personal tone.

Offer your congratulations.

Dear Sally,

When I heard through the office grapevine that you and Rob are celebrating your fifteenth wedding anniversary today, I was truly amazed!

Why do I think of the two of you as newlyweds? Could it be because you always seem so happy together, always have so much to talk to each other about, and both look so young and vivacious?

I hope you continue to savor, enjoy, and appreciate this special relationship. My warmest wishes and congratulations to both of you—Happy Anniversary.

Sincerely,

Congratulatory Letter—Birth

Offer your congratulations to the reader and his or her spouse. Add a personal comment, if appropriate.

Dear Jim,

Congratulations to you and Janet on the birth of Susannah! If your daughter inherits even a bit of your warmth, cleverness, and humor, and of Janet's charm, intelligence, and beauty, she'll be a special person indeed.

I'm looking forward to meeting the new addition to the Roberts family and to sharing your joy.

Best wishes,

Congratulatory Letter—Engagement

Give the reason for your letter and offer your best wishes.

Dear Elaine,

I've just heard that you and Bill have become engaged and plan to be married this summer. I'd like to extend my warmest wishes for great happiness together.

Add a personal comment, and close with your congratulations.

I see now why you've been looking so radiant lately. Congratulations!

Best wishes,

Congratulatory Letter—Marriage

Offer your congratulations.

Add a personal comment.

Wish the couple good luck.

Dear Tom,

Congratulations on your recent marriage! I want to wish you and your new wife a long and happy future together.

When my secretary told me your good news, she also told me a statistic she had just read—married people are considered 50% more stable and effective at their jobs. I told her there's never been concern on my part about you—you couldn't be a more efficient and desirable employee if you tried!

Best of luck.

Sincerely,

Letter Expressing Get-Well Wishes

Explain how you found out the person was ill.

Express your regrets. Offer to call or visit, if appropriate. Add a personal comment.

Offer assistance.

Dear Randy,

When I called your office this morning to talk about our next order, your secretary told me you were ill and would be out for at least a month.

I'm sorry to hear you're not feeling well, and I hope it's nothing serious! Are you up to a phone call or visit? Perhaps I could bring you some of those British mysteries you enjoy reading.

If there's anything at all I can do for you, please let me know. Get well soon!

Best wishes,

Letter Expressing Sympathy

Dear _____ :

Explain the reason for the note and express sympathy.

I read in the <u>Times</u> yesterday that your father died and I want to express my sincerest sympathy.

Add a personal comment.

I know from our many talks how close you were to him. I imagine his loss will be profoundly difficult for you.

Offer to do what you can to help.

If you need to talk, or if there is anything at all I can do for you now, please call me.

Best wishes,

Thank You Letter

Dear Friends,

Give the reason for the thanks.

I really dreaded going into the hospital last week to have my tonsils removed. I had heard that when an adult has this operation, the recuperation period can be very tedious and uncomfortable.

Explain how your colleagues' efforts made you feel.

Well, what I heard was right! But the kindness and attention of you, my colleagues in the accounting department, really made things a lot more pleasant.

Describe what was done.

Your visits, gifts, cards, and funny poems and stories really gave me a lift. And they impressed me, too—when did you all find the time in our chaotic office to prepare such great surprises?

Express your appreciation once again.

I appreciate you all so much—and I can't wait to get back to work next week to thank you in person!

With great affection,

Invitation Letter

Dear _____ :

Give the reason for the invitation.

I'd like you to join me and our entire staff for a kickoff party to introduce our newest line of hair accessories, ACCENTS.

Explain the plan for the evening, and when and where the event will take place.

We'll be having drinks and a buffet dinner on June 8 at The Kitchen, 316 W. 47th Street, at 7 p.m. After dinner comes the fashion show. Then, we'll dance and celebrate all night long!

Give additional details about guests, dress, etc.

Of course, the party won't be complete without you. Bring a guest, if you'd like. Dress for a gala. Plan to have a wonderful evening.

Explain how to respond to the invitation.

Please call our publicity coordinator, Julia Richmond, by June 1 to tell her whether you can attend. We're looking forward to sharing our exciting new line with you.

Best wishes,

Fund Raising Letter

Dear _____ :

Introduce yourself, if it seems helpful. Explain why you are writing.

As you probably know, I've always been too busy running Pontiac Industries to get involved with charity work. But recently, a small and very needy organization asked me for help, and after learning more about them I've had to say yes.

Explain what the organization is and why it needs your help.

The organization, Carter House, is a home run by the Community Aid Society where adolescents released from correctional facilities await placement in foster care.

These kids, aged 12 to 16, have never had any of the advantages we—and our own children—take for granted. Most were abandoned or abused by their parents, and have no family or friends who care about them. They haven't had proper diets, or medical or dental care. Most have never known love, attention, guidance, or consistency.

Make a personal appeal for help.

Please help me make their waiting time more bearable—and more productive.

Give details of what will be done with the donation.

We must help feed and clothe them, counsel them, teach them, and expose them to a world of love, culture, learning, and physical well-being.

(continued on following page)

Ask directly for what you want (money, time, etc.).	Please send me a check—it's tax-deductible, of course—for whatever you can afford. Every dollar counts. These kids really need us!
Thank the reader in advance to encourage action.	Let me thank you in advance on their behalf.
	Sincerely yours,

Job Application Cover Letter

Dear _____ :

Explain what position you're applying for and how you learned about the opening.

Your ad in the New York Times immediately caught my attention yesterday when I opened the classified section. The office-manager position described in the ad seems to be a perfect combination of the job I'm now performing and my strongest skills and talents.

Describe your current job and explain why it makes you a good candidate. Leave employment history details for your resume.

As you can see by my enclosed resume, I've been administrative assistant to the senior vice president for sales at Creative Computers for the past five years. I coordinate the activities of our eight-member sales force, keep a schedule of orders and deliveries, edit a monthly newsletter, write and type my supervisor's correspondence, and handle expense reports for the department.

Capsulize your best talents. Explain why you are interested in changing jobs.

I've had plenty of opportunity to prove that I'm energetic, efficient, flexible, and excellent at dealing with people. I now feel that I'm ready to move into a supervisory role, one that gives me major responsibility for the operations of a small, fast-growing company like yours.

(continued on following page)

Show that you know something about the company.

I'm particularly interested in working for your company because of the remarkable success of your new Model 71A and 71C minicomputers. Your reputation as an innovative computer manufacturer is impressive.

Ask for an appointment and tell how or where you can be reached.

I would like to set up an appointment to discuss a possible career for me at Webster Electronics. You can reach me at 555-8400 between 9 a.m. and 6 p.m. I look forward to hearing from you soon.

Sincerely yours,

Interview Follow-up Letter

Dear ——————:

Convey a positive feeling about the interview.

Our meeting this morning reinforced my conviction that I would be an asset to Webster Electronics.

Remind the reader why you qualify, based on what you learned about the job.

The office-manager position you described is a challenge I know I can meet successfully. I thrive in a hectic, pressured environment and do my best work when everyone needs me at once! One thing I've learned in my job at Creative Computers is how to set clear priorities each day, and then how to change them as new problems arise that need immediate solutions.

Say what you liked about the company.

I was very impressed with your organization as you described it to me. I like to know that advancement is rapid in a growing company, and that hard work and clear thinking are rewarded with promotions and pay increases.

Thank the reader for his or her time, and mention the next meeting.

Thank you for your time, your enthusiasm, and the enlightening education about Webster Electronics. I am looking forward to my meeting with Ms. Block next Tuesday.

Sincerely,

Letter of Reference

Dear _____ :

Explain why you are referring this person.

I'm pleased to write you about Ellen Brooks and the wonderful job she does here as a sales department administrative assistant. I'm willing to help her find a job outside our company only because she's too bright and capable to be held back, and there's no place here for her to move up.

Say what he or she has done that was outstanding.

Ellen took over her position five years ago, and I've watched as she changed this environment from one of disorganization to one in which everything is accomplished calmly and efficiently.

Describe special abilities and talents.

She always seems to know what has to be done, when to do it, and how to deal with an angry customer or a harried sales representative.

Give details about past performance.

The monthly bulletins she created two years ago on sales activity and product information have increased the sales force's feeling of friendly competition. We all push a little harder now to see ourselves named "Sales Rep of the Month" or "Company High-Roller."

Show how highly you regard his or her work.

If you hire Ellen, you'll be adding a levelheaded, hard-working, and creative woman to your staff.

Sincerely yours,

Introduction Letter

Dear _____ :

Tell whom you are introducing.

I'm writing to tell you about Eric Diamond, a former student of mine. I'm hoping you can make time to see him, in regard to a position with your firm, next month when he's in New York.

Explain how you know the person, and tell what he or she does well.

Eric was one of the most gifted students I've ever had the privilege to teach. His sense of line, structure, and design is astounding in someone with his limited experience. I imagine he'll be one of our best new architects in the future.

Give pertinent facts about this person's experience.

Eric graduated with honors. While he was attending school, he held down a job as a draftsman in order to pay his tuition. So you can see that he's hard working as well as gifted.

If the reader is not interested, ask him or her to still help the person in some way.

If you don't have room for him within your own firm, maybe you could guide him elsewhere. I think, however, that once you spend time with him and see his portfolio, you'll want very much to keep him for yourself!

Close on a personal note.

Best regards to Meg and the kids. Why don't we get together when I come in this summer for my annual visit?

Sincerely yours,

Letter Requesting an Appointment

Dear _____:

Open creatively to get the reader's interest. Make clear what your interest is.

I recently read a newspaper article that said 72% of college graduates go into the job market without a clear idea of what they want to do for a living. I was amazed to see that; since the age of 16, I've been planning to become an advertising art director. My inspiration, you'll be interested to know, was your agency's campaign for the Volkswagen Beetle!

Give highlights of your background as it pertains to the company you want to deal with. Leave details for your resume.

I am majoring in advertising communications at the School of Visual Arts and have kept a portfolio of my assignments and my own concept work for four years. For the past five summers, I've worked in offices where I could learn more about layout and design. For three years, I was a summer trainee in the Time/Life art department, where I executed pasteups and mechanicals for the magazine and film divisions. Descriptions of my other jobs appear on the enclosed resume.

Ask for what you want. If you're interested in a job, say when you will be available.

I'll be graduating this June and will be ready to work full-time right away. Since your Volkswagen campaign was my inspiration, my highest ambition is to work for you. I'd like a chance to show you my portfolio and talk with you about how I can realize my goal.

Explain how and when you can be reached.

I hope to hear from you soon. You can reach me at 555-2471 on any weekday until noon, when my classes begin.

Thank you very much.

Sincerely yours,

Letter Refusing an Appointment

Dear _____ :

Always thank the person for expressing interest.

Thank you for sending me your resume last week. I appreciate your interest in our company and I'm impressed with your extensive knowledge of the industry.

State why you must refuse.

Unfortunately, we're not hiring right now. We have just finished a rather hectic month in which we added eight writers to our staff. I can't take the time right now to meet with you because I'm very busy training these new employees.

Say what you plan to do with letter and resume, and what he or she should do.

I will keep your resume in our active file in case our needs change. I suggest you check back with me next October.

Encourage the reader in another direction.

Best of luck with your job search.

Sincerely yours,

Letter Granting a Personal Interview

Dear _____ :

Tell the person you want to arrange a meeting.

Yes! I would like to meet you. In fact, after going over your resume last night, I was surprised we haven't already met. Our career paths have zigzagged, yet not crossed, at three different companies in ten years.

Explain why.

I must caution you, however, that although we are hiring four new regional managers, none of these spots is in New York. If you're open to the idea of relocation, let's get together next week to discuss it.

Mention the person's background and what appeals to you.

I like your background and I like what I've heard about you—I've already done some discreet checking into your reputation and track record.

Ask the person to call so you can set up an interview.

Why don't you give me a call if you're interested in a next step?

Sincerely yours,

Letter Commemorating an Employee's Anniversary of Service

Dear _____ :

Explain the reason for the letter. Use a warm tone.

This Friday will mark ten years since you've joined us. It just doesn't seem possible, does it?

Reminisce about the person's time with the company.

I have to smile when I remember that I almost didn't hire you because your degree in history didn't seem right for a manufacturing company. I'm really glad you convinced me to take a chance on you. Your achievements and advancement over the years have proven you were right!

Congratulate the employee on the anniversary and thank him or her for the hard work over the years.

Congratulations on this important anniversary, and thank you for continuously giving so much of yourself to this company. You are truly admired and respected by all your superiors and colleagues for the high quality of your work, the generosity of your spirit, and your good nature and good humor.

Close with good wishes for the future.

I hope you're looking forward to an equally happy and successful future with us!

Sincerely,

Letter Welcoming a New Employee

Dear ——————— :

Give a warm and personal welcome.

I'm pleased to welcome you to the staff of Western Computers. Although we haven't met, the managers who persuaded me to hire you (despite our moratorium on new employees) have certainly made me aware of your abilities.

Describe why your company is a good place to work and what you look for in an employee.

Although we're a large company in size, we're a small company in that we care about our employees as people. We look to hire intelligent, stable, and enthusiastic workers who see a long-term future with this company, instead of considering us simply a stepping-stone in their careers.

Set up a meeting. End on an enthusiastic note.

I'd like you to come in to meet me at 11:00 on Monday so I can welcome you personally and see what all the fuss was about!

Sincerely yours,

Congratulatory Letter—Promotion

Explain the reason for the note.

Tell your feelings about the promotion.

Encourage the reader and show confidence.

Dear _____ :

Congratulations on your recent promotion to New York Sales Administrator. Although you and I have met infrequently, I'm aware of your excellent work record through regular reviews with your department heads.

When they suggested you for this position, I was comfortable with and confident about the idea.

I'd like to offer you my best wishes for continued success at Webster. I know you'll do a remarkable job.

Sincerely yours,

Congratulatory Letter—New Position

Dear _____ :

Explain the reason for your letter.

I read in the trade papers today that you've just been named to the newly created position of newsletter editor at Mead Industries. Congratulations!

Include personal details. Say why you feel the person deserves the position.

The last time we spoke, you told me how much you enjoyed developing the employee newsletter but you wished you didn't have to shoehorn it in among all your other duties. I know that now you'll really be able to make it shine! It speaks highly of you and your abilities that Mead would give you an important new project like that on a full-time basis.

Close with good wishes for the future.

The newsletter sounds like a perfect vehicle for your talents and your special brand of creativity. Congratulations again!

Sincerely yours,

Letter of Resignation

State that you are resigning and when. Use a rather formal style.

If possible, state that your association with the company was a positive one. Give your reason for leaving.

Offer to help train your replacement.

Dear _____:

This letter will serve as official notice that I am leaving my position with Henderson on Friday, May 1.

My four years as a sales rep with Henderson have been satisfying and successful and I hope you feel I was a valuable employee. As you know, I was ready for a managerial role and none was available without relocation. For this reason only, I have decided to take a management position with another company.

I have the highest regard for Henderson and want to maintain the lines of communication between us. If you would like me to help select and train my replacement, I'd be happy to do so.

Very truly yours,

Interoffice Memorandum

When communicating within the company, always use the headings "to," "from," "date," and "subject."

Introduce the subject matter, and provide all pertinent details.

If a response is required, tell who should be contacted, how, and by what date.

The memo should conclude with any additional instructions or recommendations.

To: The Staff
From: Harold Watkins, President
Date: November 30, 1985
Subject: Holiday Party

This year, we will hold our annual holiday celebration at The Oaks Country Club on December 23 at 7:30 p.m. It will be a formal dinner-dance for all our employees, clients, and spouses or special guests.

Please join us for a festive evening. It will give me a special opportunity to thank you for all your contributions to our best year ever! Call Debbie White at extension 3821 by December 15 to let her know whether you'll be there.

By the way, take December 24 off this year as an extra vacation day. This way you can eat, drink, and dance into the night with us.

Minutes of Meeting

In the heading, give the name of the group or company and the date. Tell who was in charge, who attended, and who was absent.

Minutes of the meeting of the Carter House Executive Committee
September 4, 1983
Presiding: Patrick Hammond
Present: Joy Brown
           Ray Franklin
           Elaine Schwartz
Absent: Sheila Jayson
           Barbara Jean Montana

Report the time, the place, and the reading and approval of past minutes.

The monthly meeting of the Carter House Executive Committee was called to order by Mr. Hammond at 11 a.m. in the conference room. The minutes of the meeting of August 1 were read by Mr. Franklin and approved.

Describe the main discussion and outcome.

The main discussion of the meeting concerned the fund-raising drive that began on July 12 and is being chaired by Ms. Montana. She was not available to give her report personally, but had sent along the important figures for our discussion.

Give detailed financial information.

So far we have raised $4,578 from the July mailing. We have collected an additional $6,754 from the Executive Mailing to Company Presidents. Ms. Montana projects an additional $5,000 from this effort by mid-December.

Describe plans for the next meeting. Tell where and when it will be held.	We will have a report from Sheila Jayson on our upcoming Carter House Dinner Dance at our next meeting, to be held on October 10, at 11 a.m., in the conference room.
Report additional points discussed and their outcome.	Joy Brown reported that four trampolines and six sets of "Heavy Hands" were donated for our new gym by Something Physical Exercise Studio. It was agreed that she should thank Candy Benjamin for the donation and invite her to our dinner dance as a guest.
Report the time the meeting was adjourned.	The meeting was adjourned at 11:54 a.m.
The minutes should be signed by the person who wrote them.	Respectfully submitted,

Regular Telegram

Telegrams and mail-grams often are used instead of letters to convey importance and urgency, and to get the reader's attention. They must be brief and concise. Omit all unnecessary words, but be sure the meaning is still clear.

Your appointment 8PM Tuesday June 28 changed to same day 1PM Excelsior Hotel. Confirm receipt this message with Mr. Jones at 224-8984.

Night or Mailgram

Since the cost for night telegrams and mailgrams is usually based on one charge for the first 100 words, you can send more information and be more descriptive than when sending a regular telegram. Still, be brief and concise and include only necessary points.

Chuck Jones whom you're interviewing for Branch Mgr. for Chicago spot has BSEE from Princeton. Currently with ABM as Branch Mgr. In Chicago for five years, 100% performance each year, ranked #3 in country. Prior to ABM four years Americo. Current salary 50K, total comp package '82 was 80K. Will be in your office for interview Friday, the 26 at 9AM. Hope you're pleased.

New Product Announcement

Re: COLORBRITE Pens

Tell what your product is and what it does—and how it is different from other products.

Let your customers express themselves with COLORBRITE—the elegant new ballpoint pen that offers something unique: a choice of eight distinct designs. There is a COLORBRITE pen for every taste and every mood.

Tell the reader how the product will be marketed. Mention any special features.

Each COLORBRITE pen is blister-packed on a full color card that demands attention, with full visibility of each design. An attractive display rack is available for counter or wall use—keep it close to your register.

Suggest how the product can be highlighted.

Feature COLORBRITE as a party favor. Feature it as a stocking stuffer. Feature it for Mother's Day, Father's Day, Valentine's Day, Christmas. Feature it every day!

Mention the cost, highlighting your product's value, and coupling it with additional selling features.

Everyone will want to buy one—for themselves—for others—for gifts. And here's the incredible bonus—a pen so beautiful and so finely made, yet you can retail it for under $2.50!

Tell who is manufacturing the product—why the manufacturer is good, reliable, or well-known. Offer additional selling points.

We are COLORTUNE Products of New York, one of the most experienced manufacturers in the industry today, and we have designed our product with every feature you look for in a quality pen. The COLORBRITE is shaped to fit the hand comfortably. It is precision molded. It features a long-lasting replaceable universal cartridge. And we've added a new dimension—glorious, colorful, distinctive designs that make each pen a true work of art!

We've given you the pen for the '80's—the age of individuality—the pen to reflect our times.

Restate a phrase or idea from the opening, and recommend the product to the reader.

Now, offer it to your customers and let them express themselves—with COLORBRITE.

New Employee Announcement

Give the new employee's name and responsibilities.	Bonnie North will be joining us Monday as a senior sales representative for the Wall Street area.
Describe his or her previous job and performance record.	She comes to us from Chicago, where she was a successful sales representative for Paramount Industries for eight years. For six of those years, she was the No. 1 salesperson in her district.
Explain whom he or she will work for or with, or will replace. If appropriate, say why.	She'll be sharing the Wall Street territory with Ed Manning, who, because of explosive sales growth in that area, has been doing more work than should be expected of anyone!
Ask the staff to welcome the new employee, and express confidence in his or her success.	Please join us in welcoming Bonnie and helping her feel comfortable with her new city and company. We're sure she'll be a great asset to our company.

Job Vacancy Announcement

Re: Senior Marketing Assistant's Position

Announce the new position.

We're pleased to announce that we are creating the new position of senior marketing assistant to help Michael Whitman with the Flamingo account.

Detail the qualifications and the salary. Give an example of what kind of employee could fill the position.

We are looking for an applicant with at least two years of experience in sales or marketing. A college degree is preferred. We would be interested in talking to a marketing secretary or assistant who would like to move up in both salary and responsibility. The starting salary for this position will be between $15,000 and $19,000, depending on education and experience.

Explain when interviewing will start or give an application deadline. Tell how to apply.

We will begin interviewing to fill this spot on Tuesday, March 19. If you are interested, or if you know of someone who might be qualified, contact Loren Guida in Personnel at extension 317.

New Service Announcement

Re: Mealtime in Paris Catering Service

Explain the reason for the announcement.

Mealtime in Paris, one of the most popular and respected restaurants in Midtown, is pleased to announce the start of our new office catering service.

Describe what you're offering.

Now, you can have the same fine food you are used to going out for delivered to your office and served by our waiters.

Give examples of why or how the reader might use your service or product.

When you want to impress a client or thank your staff for a job well done, Mealtime in Paris can help you make it both easy and elegant. Use us for special occasions, or for daily executive luncheons.

Give details of what's available.

We'll provide everything you need—gourmet food, experienced waiters, beautiful china and linens, and even tables and chairs, if you need them.

Make a final sales pitch.

All our chefs were trained at Cordon Bleu. We can bring a touch of Paris to your office for less than it costs to order pizza!

Explain how to get additional information.

Call Paul Unca at 555-2790 for more information. We can send a price list and menu to your office, or have a personal meal planner stop by.

About the Author

Joan Harris is a management consultant and the author of several books on business-related topics. Her most recent book was *Create Your Employee Handbook—Fast and Professionally*. Ms. Harris has written and produced industrial films and documentaries, and is a former corporate recruiter in the areas of advertising and data processing.